Bicentennial Moments

Bicentennial Moments

Robert L. Hunt

THE UPPER ROOM
Nashville, Tennessee

Cover photo is Christ Church, Frederica, St. Simons Island, Georgia. Christ Church was established in 1736 by John and Charles Wesley. The present edifice was built in 1884 by Anson Green Phelps Dodge, Jr., as a memorial to his wife, Ella Ada Phelps Dodge.

Material by Hartzell Spence, appearing in "Tribute to Asbury" (Oct. 14), is quoted from "Live or Die, I Must Ride!" in *Together* magazine, August, 1958, and is used by permission of the United Methodist Publishing House.

Illustrations on pages 17, 24, 31, 46, and 67 are taken from *The Illustrated History of Methodism* by W. H. Daniels.

Illustrations on pages 56 and 64 are taken from *Cyclopaedia of Methodism* edited by Matthew Simpson.

The drawing of Harry Hosier on page 49 is owned by Zoar Methodist Church, Philadelphia, Pennsylvania, and is used by permission of the Reverend Joshua E. Licorish.

Book design: Harriette Bateman
Cover design: John Robinson
Cover transparency: Marsh Post Card Service, Jacksonville, Florida
First printing: September, 1983(10)
Second printing: April, 1984(5)
Library of Congress Catalog Card Number: 83-50524
ISBN: 0-8358-0466-6
Printed in the United States of America

Bicentennial Moments

Contents

Preface

The material in this book is designed to be used within the Sunday morning worship service each Sunday during United Methodism's bicentennial year of 1984. For three minutes each Sunday the congregation's attention is focused on some historical event or person in our denomination's past. I believe that if this material is used each Sunday for fifty-two Sundays, by the end of 1984 the average person in the pew will be familiar with some of the names and events which are significant in United Methodist history.

The idea for this book came in preparation for the celebration of the nation's bicentennial. At that time I was pastor of the Trinity United Methodist Church in New Albany, Indiana. The average attendance of the congregation each Sunday morning was 370. Wanting to find a way to use the interest people had in historical events in 1976 to educate them about the history of United Methodism, I decided to take three minutes within each Sunday morning worship service to tell about some historical event or person related to United Methodism. We called that three minute section "Bicentennial Moments." The congregation liked the idea and looked forward to that section of the worship service.

The Bicentennial Moments worked so well that the author wanted to make the idea and research available to all those who desired to initiate a similar program in 1984. Thus the material was revised and sent to The Upper Room for possible distribution.

A congregation which adopts this approach is encouraged to

substitute on the appropriate Sundays some dates or data which have meaning in the history of the local congregation.

The congregation which uses these BICENTENNIAL MOMENTS in 1984 can grow in their understanding of and appreciation for our United Methodist heritage.

Acknowledgements

I was pastor of the Trinity United Methodist Church in New Albany, Indiana, when I had the idea for this approach to the observance of the nation's Bicentennial. My mother, Mrs. Brunner Hunt of Lake Junaluska, North Carolina, did the basic research and convinced me that we would find the dates to match each week of the year. I am grateful to her for that assistance.

I wish to thank my wife, Mary Jim, and daughter Robbie, who did much of the typing.

I am grateful also to the congregation of Trinity Church, who encouraged me and were so very receptive to this segment of our morning worship services in 1976.

Christmas Conference

January 1

United Methodism celebrates its 200th anniversary this year. We will mark this bicentennial each Sunday with a brief glimpse of some of the history of our denomination.

Friday morning, ten o'clock, December 24, 1784. Sixty-three preachers are gathered in Lovely Lane Chapel in Baltimore for a Christmas Conference. During the ten-day conference, they hear three sermons each day—one at noon from Thomas Coke, one in the morning and one in the evening—and make some important decisions.

Thomas Coke is the presiding officer. The most important vote is the decision to form a separate denomination. They decide to call the new denomination the Methodist Episcopal Church. Twelve persons are ordained elders. Thomas Coke and Francis Asbury are elected general superintendents (later the title will be changed to bishop). Asbury is ordained a deacon on Saturday and an elder on Sunday. On Monday he is consecrated a general superintendent. Philip William Otterbein is one of the men who lay hands on Asbury in the consecration (later Otterbein will become a co-founder of the United Brethren Church).

The group determines their rules of discipline and discusses the establishment of a college. The conference adjourns on Sunday, January 2.

On a snowy Tuesday, two days after the conference, Asbury rides his horse fifty miles to Fairfax, Virginia. Coke goes first to Maryland to discuss the founding of Cokesbury College, and then sets out on a preaching tour.

That's the way it was 199 years ago this week for the early American Methodists.

John Wesley in Snow

January 8

United Methodists look to John Wesley as one of the spiritual giants in history. He lived in England during the eighteenth century. Service to others was one of his major concerns.

We find one example of this in his actions of January 4-9, 1785. At that time he was eighty-one years old. He wrote in his *Journal* for those dates:

> At this season we usually distribute coals and bread among the poor of the Society; but I now considered they wanted clothes as well as food; so on this and the four following days I walked through the town, and begged two hundred pounds, [$1,000.00] in order to clothe them that wanted it most; but it was hard work, as most of the streets were filled with melting snow, which often lay ankle deep, so that my feet were steeped in snow-water nearly from morning till evening. I held it out pretty well till Saturday evening, when I was laid up with a violent flux, which increased every hour, till at six in the morning, Dr. Whitehead called upon me. His first draught* made me quite easy; and three or four more perfected the cure. If he lives some years, I expect he will be one of the most eminent Physicians in Europe.

What compassion the eighty-one-year-old man had to spend five days in January going to the homes of people through the snow to beg money for the poor! As the spiritual descendants of John Wesley, we are to have great compassion also.

---

*Draught—bloodletting, a medical practice once thought effective in treating certain ailments and diseases.

Unselfish Habits of Wesley

January 15

When we are unjustly criticized, it is helpful to realize that others have had the same experience. Even John Wesley was not immune.

On January 16, 1760, Wesley wrote in his *Journal,* "One came to me, as she said, with a message from the Lord, to tell me, 'I was laying up treasures on earth, taking my ease, and minding only my eating and drinking.' I told her, 'God knew me better; and if he had sent her, he would have sent her with a more proper message.' "

Wesley's lifestyle supported his response. Rather than "laying up treasures," he gave away two hundred thousand dollars in his lifetime and died poor. In a sermon on "The Use of Money," Wesley's points were: "Gain all you can; save all you can; give all you can."

Wesley did not live a life of leisure. He rode his horse approximately five thousand miles a year for over fifty years. Often riding seventy or eighty miles a day and seldom sleeping more than six hours a night, during his lifetime he preached forty thousand sermons—an average of eight hundred sermons per year or more than fifteen each week. One week he preached fifteen times in thirteen places. Usually he began preaching at five o'clock in the morning.

In his spare time Wesley was a prolific writer, translator, and editor. He put together more than four hundred books and pamphlets.

The only comment which needs to be made about his eating and drinking habits is that he weighed 130 pounds.

Wesley lived by the rules he gave his fellow workers, "Be diligent. Never be unemployed. Never be triflingly employed. Never *while away* time: neither spend any more time at any one place than is strictly necessary."

Our lives are to be characterized by personal disciplines also.

Wesley and Georgia

January 22

In his early thirties John Wesley came to the colony of Georgia as a missionary to the Indians. As it turned out, he spent most of his time with colonists rather than with Indians. In time he became disillusioned about his efforts in the New World.

December 22, 1737. Slightly less than two years after his arrival, Wesley leaves America to return to England. On the voyage home, on January 24, 1738, he writes in his *Journal,*

> "I went to America, to convert the Indians; but oh! who shall convert me! Who, what is he that will deliver me from this evil heart of unbelief? I have a fair summer religion. I can talk well; nay, and believe myself, while no danger is near; but let death look me in the face, and my spirit is troubled. Nor can I say "To die is gain!"

Even back in England, Wesley feels no better. He writes,

> It is now two years and almost four months since I left my native country, in order to teach the Georgian Indians the nature of Christianity; but what have I learned myself in the mean time? Why, (what I the least of all suspected,) that I who went to America to convert others, was never myself converted to God.

Wesley's spiritual depression continued. It would be May before the turning point would come at Aldersgate. In the early part of 1738 there is no indication of the spiritual giant Wesley would become later.

Augusta
SOUTH
CAROLINA
Santee R.
Savannah R.
Edisto R.
Ashley R.
Cooper R.
UCHEES
YAMASSEES
Combahee R.
Charleston
Beaufort
Port Royal Id.
Ogeechee R.
Ebenezer
Savannah
Edisto Id.
St. Helena Sd.
St. Helena Id.
Charleston Har.
Port Royal Entrance
Hilton Head Id.
Cannouchee R.
Ossabaw Id.
Altamaha R.
St. Catharine's Id.
OCEAN
Darien
Sapelo Id.
Frederica
Bloody Marsh
St. Simon's Id.
English Battery
Satilla R.
Ft. Andrew
Cumberland Id.
Ft. William
St. Marys R.
Talbot Id.
Ft. George
FLORIDA
St. John's R.
St. Augustine
33
32
31
30
MILES 20 40 60 80 100 120 140 160

Concern About Social Issues

January 29

John Wesley had strong feelings about the social issues of his day. He wrote in his *Journal* on February 3, 1753,

> I visited one in the Marshalsea Prison, a nursery of all manner of wickedness. O shame to man, that there should be such a place, such a picture of hell upon earth! And shame to those who bear the name of Christ, that there should need any prison at all in Christendom!

On another occasion he wrote,

> In returning to London, I read the Life of the late Tsar, Peter the Great. Undoubtedly he was a Soldier, a General, and a Statesman, scarce inferior to any; but why was he called a Christian? What has Christianity to do either with deep dissimulation or savage cruelty?

Wesley took a strong stand against slavery. The last letter he wrote was to William Wilberforce, a leader in the fight against slavery. He encouraged him, "Go on in the name of God, and in the power of His might. . . . "

The attitude of many persons toward the poor upset Wesley. He told of two days spent visiting the sick who were poor. He saw how each of them who was well enough to crawl was working and then wrote, "So wickedly, devilishly false is that common objection, 'They are poor only because they are idle.' "

Milburn Akers, an editor for the Chicago *Sun-Times,* wrote of the conditions in England,

> Wesley, when he began his mission, was confronted by a rum-soaked, religiously indifferent, cynical people; a complacent church which had lost contact with those it was supposed to serve;

> an economic system which brutalized those it employed and a government, corrupt and inefficient, which existed only to attend the status quo.

Mr. Akers stated the influence of Wesley and his followers,

> The movement which began in the Holy Club at Oxford was a prime factor in making the slave trade illegal, in bringing about a more humane recodification of England's brutal criminal laws, in reforming its penal system and in making the lot of women and children, pitiful victims of the industrial revolution, easier.

From the beginning, Methodists have had the twofold emphasis: our relationships with others as well as our relationship with God.

Fire at Epworth Rectory

February 5

"A brand plucked from the burning." The phrase, worded a bit differently,* is engraved on one of John Wesley's portraits, and it symbolizes his mother's belief that God had a special plan for John.

February 9, 1709. The five-year-old John and his family are at home in the rectory at Epworth; his father, Samuel, is a minister in the Church of England.

The family is asleep—the older members on the ground floor and five of the children in the attic. Sleep is interrupted, however, when the thatch roof catches fire (it is thought that a parishoner set it). While John sleeps, the others escape in their nightclothes to the snow and icy wind outside.

Samuel counts his children and discovers that John is missing. He makes his way into the house through the smoke, only to find the stairway consumed by flames. As Samuel returns to the yard, John appears in the attic window. Neighbors make a human ladder, and the roof falls as they pull him through the window.

It is then that Susanna Wesley, John's mother, realizes that God has saved him for a special purpose, and she refers to him as a "brand plucked from the burning." She prays, "I do intend to be more particularly careful of the soul of this child, that Thou hast so mercifully provided for. . . ."

The fire at the Wesleys' took place 275 years ago this week, and it demonstrates eternal truth. Whether or not we are dramatically rescued from some disaster, God has a special plan for each of us. God wants to use us for the fulfillment of divine purposes.

---

*"Is not this a brand plucked out of the fire?"—Coke & Moore's *Wesley*, quoted in Telford, *The Life of John Wesley*, p.18

Whitefield in Open Air

February 12

George Whitefield, a friend of the Wesleys from Oxford days, began the practice of preaching outdoors. Coal miners from Kingswood, England, were his first audience on February 17, 1739.

It was said of George Whitefield that when he preached his voice could be heard a mile, and the singing of the audiences carried two miles. Others later said that by merely pronouncing the word "Mesopotamia" he could bring tears to the eyes of his listeners.

The authors of *The Story of Methodism* tell what happened when Whitefield began his services outside:

> If Whitefield's first open air congregation numbered two hundred, his second was just ten times as large. It was not long before he was preaching to twenty thousand people. The miners came straight from the pit to listen, and there is no picture in all the annals of that early Methodism easier to imagine than that of the white furrows that appeared on their blackened cheeks, as they listened spellbound, and the tears came coursing down.

George Whitefield began urging John Wesley to preach outdoors. Wesley's initial reaction is recorded in his *Journal,* "All my life . . . [I had been] so tenacious of every point relating to decency and order, that I should have thought the saving of souls almost a sin, if it had not been done in a church." However he took up the idea and used it extensively over the years of his ministry.

Two hundred forty-five years ago this week a new method of reaching people was started. In our generation we too are to be open to new methods of reaching persons for Christ.

Wesley's Trips to Falmouth

February 19

The impact which John Wesley and his movement had on England can be seen to some extent in three of the visits he made to Falmouth.

His first visit was on July 4, 1745, when his movement was just getting started. During his call on a sick woman, a mob gathered outside the door and called for him to come out. In the mob were several privateers, men hired by the government to harass enemy shipping. When Wesley did not come, some of the men ripped the doors from their hinges. Although Wesley thought his life was not worth an "hour's purchase," he faced them with his usual poise. Wesley asked for the chance to speak and held off the mob with words until "one or two of their captains turned about and swore, 'not a man should touch him [Wesley].' "

His second visit was ten years later on September 2, 1755. No rioting took place on that trip. He preached to a "deeply attentive" congregation.

He came to Falmouth the last time on August 18, 1789. In his *Journal* he noted that the tide had turned.

> High and low now lined the street from one end of the town to the other, out of stark love and kindness, gaping and staring as if the King were going by. In the evening I preached on the smooth top of the hill, at a small distance from the sea. . . . God moved wonderfully on the hearts of the people, who all seem to know the day of their visitation.

We celebrate the changes brought in human lives and in communities touched by John Wesley.

Wesley's Death

February 26

John Wesley preached the last of his 42,400 sermons on February 23, 1791, at Leatherhead near London. His text was, "Seek ye the Lord while he may be found, call ye upon him while he is near."

On the following day he wrote a letter to William Wilberforce, who was leading the struggle against slavery. He encouraged Wilberforce,

> Unless God has raised you up for this very thing, you will be worn out by the opposition of men and devils; but, *if God be for you, who can be against you?* Are all of them together stronger than God? O, *'be not weary in well-doing.'* Go on, in the name of God, and in the power of his might, till even American slavery, the vilest that ever saw the sun, shall vanish away before it. [It is significant to note that Wesley had been the earliest of the religious leaders of Great Britain to denounce slavery.]

On Thursday, February 24, at the age of eighty-eight, Wesley became ill and worsened in the following days. He frequently told those around him to pray and praise. At other times he said to them, "The best of all is, God is with us!"

At ten o'clock on Monday morning, March 2, 1791 Wesley died. His body was buried a week later at City Road Chapel. Burial was held at five o'clock in the morning because it was feared too large a crowd would assemble at a more convenient time.

During this anniversary week of Wesley's death 193 years ago, we thank God that the Spirit works through human beings to touch the lives of others and even to change the course of human history.

Circuit Riders

March 4

The heroes of early United Methodism in this country were the circuit rider preachers.

The circuit riders did not stay long in one place. Their home was their horse as they traveled from community to community and from home to home. When they were invited to sleep inside a cabin, they did. When there was no invitation, they slept outside. Barns, cabins, and fields were the only churches they had.

At the Christmas Conference in 1784, the annual salary approved for the preachers was sixty-four dollars. No minister made more than any other. In 1800 the salary was raised to eighty dollars per year, "and their travelling expenses."

A horse usually cost a year's salary, but it was necessary for a circuit rider. Horse and rider traveled through all kinds of weather, on all kinds of roads and terrain. In the relatively settled country of Maryland and Virginia, George Brown wore out eight horses in two years.

Poverty and traveling made marriage impractical. Of the eighty-four Methodist preachers in Virginia in 1809, only three were married.

When Thomas Ware went to east Tennessee in 1787, he described himself with these words,

> I set out for my field of labor poorly clad and nearly penniless, but happy in God. In the Holston country there was but little money and clothing was very dear. My coat was worn through at the elbows; and I had not a whole undergarment left; and as for boots, I had none. But my health was good, and I was finely mounted. . . .

Bishop Asbury crossed the mountains in Tennessee in 1790 and reported, "I found the poor preachers indifferently clad, with emaciated bodies, and subject to hard fare; yet I hope they are rich in faith."

Today we remember with respect and admiration the early circuit riders.

A Challenging Mission

March 11

The preachers at the 1784 Christmas Conference asked themselves, "What may we reasonably believe to be God's design in raising up Methodist preachers?" The answer written into the minutes was, "To reform the continent, and to spread scriptural holiness over these lands." That was a challenging mission!

The men who made and accepted that challenge were few in number but intense in conviction. They sacrificed much to fulfill their mission.

Each circuit rider was assigned to a specific territory, and it was his goal to reach each community in his area once a month. The territories, however, were often the size of half a state and yet the riders did their best.

They went to the people. One preacher reported coming upon a man unpacking his wagon. The circuit rider introduced himself. "What!" exclaimed the settler, "Another Methodist preacher! Have you found us already?" The settler said he had left Virginia and Georgia to get away from the Methodists.

When we study the conditions in which those circuit riders lived we wonder how they survived. The answer is that many did not. Prior to 1847 approximately half of the preachers died before reaching the age of thirty. Of the first 672 preachers whose records were kept in full, two-thirds of them died before they were able to render twelve years of service. Just one less than 200 died within their first five years of service.

One of the traditions of annual conference has been to open the conference with the singing of the hymn, "And Are We Yet Alive?" In the light of United Methodist history, this song carries stirring significance.

Charles Wesley

March 18

Charles Wesley made many contributions to the Wesleyan movement. He was four years younger than his brother John, but their lives were similar in many ways. They grew up in the same home, attended Oxford University, participated in the Holy Club, spent time in the New World, and went through deep spiritual experiences within the same week.

The Wesley brothers published a new hymn book almost annually for several years. As time went on, Charles wrote much more than his brother, and today he is known primarily as a writer of hymns. At thirty he wrote, "Hark! the Herald Angels Sing." He was thirty-nine when he wrote "Love Divine, All Loves Excelling." At the age of forty-one he wrote "O For a Thousand Tongues to Sing."

Charles Wesley blended deep religious insight with poetic genius, classical learning, and wide reading. In his generation he set the masses to singing. The Wesleys seemed to have assumed that Christians would want to sing. When a congregation was not singing, they took for granted that there was something spiritually wrong.

Charles Wesley spent the last seventeen years of his life in London and died on March 29, 1788, 196 years ago this month.

Even on his deathbed he wanted to write hymns. Pen and paper were brought to his bedside, and his wife took down the lines. His last words were, "I'll praise. . . . "

The Lambuth Family

March 25

Over a hundred years ago a young school teacher in Mississippi was deeply moved by a missionary's sermon. She put five dollars and a note in the collection basket. The note read, "I give five dollars and myself." Her name was Mary I. McClellan.

On October 20, 1853, she married James William Lambuth. He had had an interesting background. It was while his father John R. Lambuth was preaching at a camp meeting that he heard of the birth of James William. He said, "I dedicate this child to God as a foreign missionary. . . . "

James William Lambuth had studied law and medicine, but neither of them had satisfied him. So he had decided to become a missionary. On March 25-26 (130 years ago today) he was attending a missionary institute at Richmond, Virginia. The Methodist churches in Richmond collected fifteen hundred dollars for his mission to China.

While the Lambuths were serving in China, the Civil War cut off their funds from the United States. Mary took in boarders to meet expenses. She wrote an astronomy book in Chinese when she saw how the Chinese feared an eclipse of the sun. She began a crusade to end the Chinese custom of binding the feet of girls.

The children of the Lambuths became missionaries. Walter Russell Lambuth served in China and Japan before opening missionary work in Africa, South America, and Europe. He was elected a bishop in 1910. Nora and Robert also served as missionaries to China. The grandchildren who became missionaries included Margarite and Nettie.

Many families stand out in our United Methodist heritage, and one of the most dedicated was the Lambuth family.

Tobias Gibson

April 1

It is difficult for us to imagine the efforts that some of our ancestors put forth to minister to others. Consider the example of Tobias Gibson.

Gibson served for eight years as a preacher in North Carolina, South Carolina, and Georgia. At the end of eight years his health was so bad that he was left without appointment with liberty to travel where he pleased.

The assignment was meant to make his load lighter. However he undertook an arduous effort. He decided to go to the Natchez country along the Mississippi River to establish Methodism there. He traveled six hundred miles on horseback to the Cumberland River, then by skiff to the Ohio River and to the Mississippi River. He finally took passage on a flatboat to Natchez where he arrived in March, 1799.

He preached almost every day—in schoolhouses, in private dwellings, on flatboats, in the woods. To meet his appointments he swam creeks, traveled in all sorts of weather, and sometimes camped out at night.

At the end of the first year sixty persons had become Methodists. The second year the membership increased to eighty and by the end of the third year to one hundred. The next year the rolls were pruned back to eighty-five.

In 1802 his health began to deteriorate more, but he continued. Other helpers joined him. He preached for the last time on January 1, 1804, and died on April 5 of that year, 180 years ago this week.

"We marvel at the purpose" which held these persons to their courses in spite of all kinds of obstacles. Their devotion is an inspiration to us.

Letter of Thomas Taylor

April 8

Sometimes new steps are taken very slowly. Consider the matter of Methodist immigrants in New York City, who wanted Mr. Wesley to send a Methodist preacher to this continent as their pastor.

On April 11, 1768, Thomas Taylor, formerly an Irish Methodist who had come to New York City, wrote Mr. Wesley about the development of a Methodist congregation. He stated,

> We want an able and experienced preacher—one who has both gifts and graces necessary for the work [sounds like a modern Pastor-Parish Relations Committee]. God has not despised the day of small things. There is real work in many hearts, by the preaching of Mr. Webb and Mr. Embury; but although they are both useful, and their hearts in the work, they want [lack] many qualifications necessary for such an undertaking, where they have none to direct them. And the progress of the gospel here depends much upon the qualifications of the preachers.

Mr. Taylor ended by saying,

> With respect to the money for payment of a preacher's passage over, if they could not procure it, we would sell our coats and shirts, and pay it. I most earnestly beg an interest in your prayers, and trust you and many of our brethren will not forget the Church in this wilderness.

Wesley reported the appeal at the next conference of his ministers, but no one was sent because of the urgent need for more preachers at home. The appeal was presented again the following year, August 1769, and two men accepted the challenge. Richard Boardman and Joseph Pilmoor were sent to New York.

Sometimes events move slowly. Taylor wrote Wesley 216 years ago this week, but it was almost one and one-half years before there were any visible results. It may take time, but God uses people who are willing to sell "coats and shirts" to advance divine causes on earth.

Richard Boardman

Joseph Pilmoor

Black Minister Laura Lange

April 15

Apparently the first black woman to be ordained in the Methodist Episcopal Church was Laura J. Lange.

She was born in St. Matthews, Kentucky, on May 11, 1880. She attended seminary at Garrett Biblical Institute and did additional study at Northwestern University.

Bishop Theodore S. Henderson ordained her a deacon at Cincinnati, Ohio, on April 18, 1926. The Reverend Laura Lange was ordained an elder by Bishop Matthew W. Clair in 1936. She served churches in Kentucky and Indiana.

Since 1926 several hundred other women have become clergy persons. A study published in 1980 indicated that there were 838 women under clerical appointment in The United Methodist Church then. Of the women who responded to a survey and were ordained, 50 percent had been ordained elders after 1976 and 87 percent (555 women) were pastors in local congregations.

Twenty-eight percent of the United Methodist clergywomen were married to ministers, making clergy couples a significant factor in our ministerial ranks.

We are proud of the new opportunities available to women in our country and within The United Methodist Church. In 1980 a woman was elected a bishop. Bishop Marjorie Matthews has been serving the Wisconsin Area.

We remember today the ordination of the Reverend Laura Lange, who probably was the first black woman to be ordained a deacon in The Methodist Episcopal Church—fifty-eight years ago this week.

Death of Samuel Wesley

April 22

Samuel Wesley, the father of John and Charles Wesley, was a person of strong convictions.

In his early years he served as chaplain on a man-o-war. Could that have been one of the influences which led him later to become the advocate of a comprehensive scheme for foreign missions?

When Samuel Wesley was rector at one parish, a nobleman supported the church but lived a loose life. When Mr. Wesley realized the nobleman would not change, he resigned so that he would not have to live dependent upon a non-Christian benefactor.

When Samuel Wesley went to Epworth, he felt the people were ignorant and godless. He told them how he saw them, but they did not appreciate his honesty. Finally, however, they learned to respect him, and he served the parish for 38 years.

Two statements from Wesley's deathbed were important to his sons. He said to Charles, "Be steady. The Christian faith will surely revive in this kingdom; you shall see it, though I shall not." And to John, he said, "The inward witness, son, the inward witness—that is the proof, the strongest proof, of Christianity."

At the time John Wesley did not understand what his father meant. However, the witness of the Spirit later became one of the themes of his ministry.

Samuel Wesley died on April 25, 1735, 249 years ago this week. We pay tribute today to this man, who was not known for his tact, but who helped to mold the lives of his children and through two of his sons made an outstanding contribution to Christian history.

Garrettson Returns from Nova Scotia

April 29

One of the colorful preachers of early Methodism was Freeborn Garrettson.

At the 1784 Christmas Conference a mission to Nova Scotia was established and Freeborn Garrettson was given the appointment. He arrived in Nova Scotia in the winter of 1785, and within two years he had built a church of five hundred.

On May 1, 1787, Garrettson returned from Nova Scotia to attend conference in Baltimore. John Wesley wanted him to become superintendent of the work in Nova Scotia, and Garrettson anticipated returning. Garrettson recorded his reaction to what happened, "I was astonished, when the appointments were read, to hear my name mentioned to preside in the Peninsula [Maryland]." So the American superintendents did not follow the desire of Mr. Wesley.

Garrettson later worked in the area north of New York City. With twelve other preachers, he opened the way from New York to the Canadian border and as far west as Niagara.

Freeborn Garrettson is remembered in part for the way he dealt with the issue of slavery. Soon after he became a minister he inherited some slaves from his father. He was unaware of the moral implications of slavery and accepted the heritage. Soon his preaching seemed to grow weaker. Garrettson knew there was a problem, but he could not put his finger on the issue. He became distressed and finally called his family together for a session of prayer. As he stood before them he seemed to hear an inner voice say, "It is not right for you to keep your fellow creatures in bondage; you must let the oppressed go free." Garrettson immediately freed the slaves and in his own words, "I was now at liberty to proceed in worship. . . . All my dejection, and that melancholy gloom which preyed upon me, vanished in a moment, and a divine sweetness ran through my whole frame."

William McKendree Elected Bishop

May 6

One of the adjutants in the Revolutionary War was William McKendree. He served in the commissary department of the Continental Army and was present at the surrender of Cornwallis at Yorktown.

Six months after the war, he was converted under the preaching of John Easter, and a year later he was received on trial as a minister. He advanced rapidly and in 1799 was sent west to supervise the work in Kentucky, Ohio, Tennessee, western Virginia and part of Illinois. Within ten years, Methodism in that area had fifteen thousand members and was divided into five districts.

In May, 1808, McKendree was in Baltimore for the general conference. He was invited to preach at one of the local churches, and he accepted. When he began preaching, he felt uncomfortable in the city church. He was dressed in frontier clothes, and as he preached, his red undershirt began popping through between his vest and trousers. As he continued preaching, he warmed to the occasion. In spite of his frontier appearance, his personal magnetism captivated the audience. Francis Asbury was present and noted that the service would make William McKendree a bishop.

On May 12, 1808, 176 years ago this week, the delegates to the general conference began balloting to elect a bishop. Of the 128 votes cast, McKendree received 95 to become the first American-born bishop.

Susanna Wesley

May 13

The most prominent mother in United Methodism is Susanna Wesley, the mother of John and Charles Wesley. She had nineteen children, although ten died.

Because there were no schools for small children, she was responsible for educating hers. Susanna was a good teacher. She was patient, but firm, and she imparted a love of learning to her students.

At the age of one each child was taught "to fear the rod and cry softly." As soon as the children could speak, they were taught the Lord's Prayer, which was repeated each morning and evening. As the children grew older, they were taught other prayers and scriptures. Also a young child in the Wesley home was taught to distinguish the Sabbath from other days. No one was permitted to take God's name in vain, curse, swear, or use rude names.

Once a week Susanna took each child aside for one hour to talk privately about their spiritual life.

At the age of five each child was inducted into the fellowship of learning by mastering the alphabet. From then on the child attended school in the home from nine o'clock until noon and from two o'clock until five each weekday.

Even with all the responsibilities of being a mother, teacher, and minister's wife, Susanna Wesley still took time for daily devotions. When she was about thirty years old, she adopted the practice of taking an hour each morning and evening for solitary meditations. Later she added time at noon.

On this Mother's Day, we honor Susanna Wesley as a teacher, spiritual leader, wife, and mother.

Aldersgate

May 20

On Wednesday, May 24, 1738, John Wesley wrote in his *Journal*,

> I think it was about five this morning that I opened my Testament on those words: "There are given unto us exceeding great and precious promises, even that ye should be partakers of the divine nature" (2 Peter 1:4). Just as I went out, I opened it again on those words: "Thou art not far from the kingdom of God." In the afternoon I was asked to go to St. Paul's. The anthem was, "Out of the deep have I called unto Thee, O Lord. . . . "
>
> In the evening I went very unwillingly to a society in Aldersgate-street, where one was reading Luther's preface to the Epistle to the Romans. About a quarter before nine, while he was describing the change which God works in the heart through faith in Christ, I felt my heart strangely warmed. I felt I did trust in Christ, Christ alone, for salvation; and an assurance was given me, that he had taken away *my* sins, even *mine*, and saved *me* from the law of sin and death.

This Christian experience was the turning point in Wesley's life. Ever since his trip to Georgia, Wesley had known that something was missing. He had questioned, searched, and prayed for months until finally he found in his Aldersgate experience that for which he was looking. For a short time John Wesley had problems with the old ways of thinking, but after May 24, 1738, the old inner torment diminished, and it was not mentioned again after 1739.

John Wesley was increasingly empowered by God to touch the lives of others. Even without the advantage of the mass communication techniques we have today, God was able to use the life of Wesley to influence both British and American history.

Today we celebrate the Christian experience that came to John Wesley 246 years ago this week.

Jesse Lee Assigned to New England

May 27

Jesse Lee was another of the interesting personalities in our United Methodist heritage.

Lee was converted just prior to the Revolutionary War. He was drafted for the army while on a preaching tour in North Carolina in 1780. When he refused to bear arms, he was thrown into the guardhouse. Lee refused to be quieted and preached from the guardhouse. A revival broke out among the troops. A colonel begged Lee to reconsider his decision not to bear arms. He still refused but agreed to drive the baggage wagon. He continued to preach as long as he was in the army. He was discharged after four months.

When annual conference opened on May 28, 1789, in New York, Jesse Lee was thirty-one years old, weighed 259 pounds, and was an excellent public speaker with a ready wit. At the conference he was appointed to Stamford, Connecticut, the first town across the Connecticut border. Actually the appointment was for all New England. The appointment had been Lee's idea; Bishop Asbury had been opposed, but Lee had persuaded him to make the appointment.

Jesse Lee was successful in New England and won the respect of many persons. Eventually he was made chaplain of the United States House of Representatives. We will think about him again in July.

The appointment of Jesse Lee to New England was made 195 years ago this week. Again and again we marvel at the vision as well as dedication of our spiritual ancestors. They were willing to assume large territories and major responsibilities to fulfill their mission—"to reform the continent and spread scriptural holiness."

Philip Otterbein

June 3

Philip William Otterbein exerted a strong influence on our United Methodist heritage. He was born on June 3, 1726, and was ordained into the ministry of the German Reformed Church in 1749. He came to America in 1752 when he became pastor of a church in Lancaster, Pennsylvania. His six-year pastorate there was followed by other pastorates until he moved to Baltimore to a church in which he served for the last thirty-nine years of his life.

In his first pastorate Otterbein felt something was spiritually not right. One Sunday he preached a sermon on God's grace. After the service a parishioner questioned him about the meaning of grace. "Advice is scarce with me this day," Otterbein responded and turned away abruptly. He then went into a quiet room where he experienced an inner assurance of God's grace. That experience was deeply meaningful to him and influenced him for the rest of his life.

Otterbein's ministry became even more effective. In Baltimore his influence extended well beyond the city. When the United Brethren in Christ Church was formed in 1800, Otterbein was elected one of the two general superintendents.

Otterbein and Francis Asbury were good friends even though they were opposites in many ways. Otterbein was schooled in philosophy, logic, math, history, and theology, as well as in Greek and Roman literature. In comparison Asbury was virtually uneducated. Otterbein participated in the consecration of Asbury, the first general superintendent in the Methodist Episcopal Church.

Many great persons have had a part in making United Methodism what it is today. On this Sunday we celebrate the birth of Philip William Otterbein 258 years ago today.

Philip Otterbein and Martin Boehm

June 10

Among the early followers of Jesus a replacement for Judas Iscariot was determined by lot. When Martin Boehm was thirty-one years of age, he was chosen by lot to become the pastor of his Mennonite church. Boehm was awed by that responsibility and felt that he was a preacher with nothing to preach.

As he worked in a field one morning, the words "lost, lost" kept coming to his mind. He later wrote, "Midway in the field I could go no farther but sank behind the plough, crying, 'Lord, save me: I am lost.' . . . Like a dream old things passed away and it seemed as if I had awoke to new life, new thoughts, new faith, new love. This joy I wished to communicate to those around me. . . . "

Boehm had a message. He began to preach effectively, but he was expelled from the Mennonite Church because of what some in the church held to be deviations and errors.

On Pentecost Sunday, 1767, Boehm spoke in a barn near Lancaster, Pennsylvania. Otterbein, at that time a pastor in the German Reformed Church, was at the service and was impressed with Boehm's message and spirit. After the service he embraced Boehm and exclaimed in German, *"Wir sind Bruder!"* (We are brothers!)

In 1800 the two met with fourteen ministers near Frederick, Maryland, and formed the United Brethren in Christ Church. William Otterbein and Martin Boehm were elected general superintendents.

Otterbein and Boehm met on Pentecost Sunday 217 years ago. God blessed the work they began that day, and we are a part of their legacy.

John Seybert

June 17

Henry Seybert was a German mercenary soldier in the British Army during the Revolutionary War. After the war he married and two of his four sons grew to maturity. One of those sons was John Seybert.

Henry died when John was fifteen, and a year later Mrs. Seybert deserted her two sons.

John was raised a Lutheran, but on June 21, 1810, he attended a revival held by an Evangelical preacher and was converted. Before long Seybert was a preacher in the Evangelical Association. He was dedicated and effective but not a dynamic preacher. He enjoyed pastoral work and excelled as an administrator.

He was elected bishop in 1839. After the election he rose and walked back to one of the last pews, bowed his head and wept. Then he came forward and said, "I have promised God to be obedient and since the brethren have elected me to be overseer, I will acquiesce, but I realize that I lack that fitness for this weighty office which my older brethren possess: you must therefore pray for me and have patience with me."

Seybert became concerned about the study habits of his ministers. Once he escorted a shipment of almost twenty-four thousand books from the printing press in Pennsylvania to the frontier by means of wagon, railroad, and boat.

During his ministry he traveled 175,000 miles, preached 9,850 sermons, and made 46,000 pastoral calls.

One hundred seventy-four years ago this week John Seybert had the religious experience that changed the direction of his life.

"Brother Van"

June 24

June 30, 1872. A young man from Gettysburg, Pennsylvania, arrives in Fort Benton, Montana, and begins looking for a place to preach. At twenty-two years of age he is penniless and owes fifty dollars for the trip. When he asks for a place to preach, he is directed to the courthouse, a log shack with a leaking roof. Not satisfied to preach there, he goes to the saloon. Despite spinning roulette wheels and busy bartenders, he gets permission to preach there. The proprietor announces him, "Ladies and gentlemen, 'The Four Deuces' is happy to present, for the first time in Fort Benton, or Montana Territory, a real, genuwine preacher. Everybody keep still until he's through, and bar's closed for an hour. Go ahead, preacher."

The minister speaks and sings some hymns, including one he would make famous in the area—"Diamond in the Rough."

At the close of the service he is applauded, and a man in the crowd yells, "What's your name?"

"William Wesley Van Orsdel."

"We'll call him Brother Van for short," the man shouted.

Within two years Brother Van was riding four thousand miles each year on his circuit and becoming a legend. He converted the owner of a "hurdy-gurdy" house in Helena and reformed Virginia City's number-one drunk.

On one occasion, the stagecoach in which he was riding was robbed. The bandit frisked the passengers one by one until he reached the clergyman. Brother Van asked, "Now you wouldn't rob a poor Methodist preacher, would you?" The bandit replied, "Never mind. I'm a Methodist myself."

After fifty years Brother Van left as his monument more than one hundred churches and institutions in the Northwest.

Brother Van arrived in Montana 112 years ago this week.

Visit to George Washington

July 1

In April, 1789, George Washington was inaugurated president of the United States. On May 29 a delegation of Methodists led by Bishops Asbury and Coke met with him in New York City, to assure the new government of Methodist loyalty.

John Wesley, the spiritual founder of Methodism, had been very outspoken for King George III. Most of the preachers sent to America by Wesley had returned to England before the end of the Revolutionary War. Thus Methodists had the reputation of being pro-England. The American Methodists in 1789 wanted the new government to understand that they were supportive.

The text of the Methodist statement to President Washington stated in part:

> We, the bishops of the Methodist-Episcopal Church, humbly beg leave, in the name of our society collectively in these United States, to express to you the warm feelings of our hearts, and our sincere congratulations, on your appointment to the presidentship of these states. We are conscious from the signal proofs you have already given, that you are a friend of mankind; and under this established idea, place as full a confidence to your wisdom and integrity, for the preservation of those civil and religious liberties which have been transmitted to us by the providence of God, and the glorious revolution, as we believe, ought to be reposed in man.
>
> . . . We promise you our fervent prayers to the throne of grace, that God Almighty may endue you with all the graces and gifts of his Holy Spirit, that may enable you to fill up your important station to his glory, the good of his church, the happiness and prosperity of the United States, and the welfare of mankind.

On this Sunday prior to July 4, we pledge anew our allegiance to the ideals of our country.

Jesse Lee in Boston

July 8

In May we discussed Jesse Lee's appointment to New England. He arrived in Norwalk, Connecticut, in 1789 and began the work there. He looked first for a place to preach. He requested the use of a private home, but was denied. He asked for the use of an old deserted building, but was refused. He asked to preach in an orchard, but permission was withheld. Finally, on June 17, 1789, Lee stood under an apple tree along a public road and began preaching.

Lee traveled throughout the area and preached wherever he could—schoolhouses, courthouses, private homes, barns, or outdoors. Many people heard his message, but few responded. At the end of seven months, only three classes had been formed. Rather than pulling Methodism out of the area, however, Bishop Asbury sent three more preachers.

On July 9, 1790, Lee arrived in Boston and again began looking for a place to preach. He was refused at first, but he finally borrowed a table and placed it under an old elm tree near the center of the Common. The service on July 10 began with a congregation of four and closed with a congregation of three thousand.

Lee encountered many trials, hardships, and some persecution, but by 1810, twenty-one years after his arrival in New England, there were twenty-five-thousand Methodists in the area and 125 appointed preachers.

Lee served for a time as chaplain in the House of Representatives. Colleagues felt he was becoming too involved with the government, however, so he resigned the position after six years.

One hundred ninety-four years ago this week Jesse Lee preached his first sermon in Boston.

Robert Strawbridge

July 15

Methodist preachers were active in the New World prior to the Christmas Conference of 1784. Although they were still under the jurisdiction of John Wesley, they met from time to time even though their numbers were very small.

The first conference of Methodist preachers in colonial times was held in Philadelphia in 1773. There is some disagreement about the exact date, but Francis Asbury and Jesse Lee both wrote that the date was July 14. When the appointments were read, Robert Strawbridge was one of the preachers who received an appointment.

Strawbridge came from Ireland and settled on Sam's Creek, Frederick County, Maryland, sometime prior to 1753. As soon as he had built a cabin, he used it for a house and a church. Later he built Sam's Creek Meeting House and organized a Methodist society. Even as a lay preacher, he took it upon himself to administer the sacraments.

By 1769 Strawbridge had mapped out a wide circuit of churches. His work was effective and several of his converts became preachers also, including Freeborn Garrettson. At the time of the first conference 500 of the 1,160 Methodists in the colonies were from the area under the influence of Strawbridge. When Strawbridge died, probably in 1781, approximately four-fifths of all the members of Methodist societies were in Maryland and to the south where his ministry had extended.

Strawbridge was a man of strong convictions and independence, and his determined spirit sometimes worried Francis Asbury and others. Learning of the death of Strawbridge, Asbury wrote, "He is no more; upon the whole I am inclined to think the Lord took him away in judgment because he was in a way to do hurt to his cause. . . . " But Asbury also acknowledged the good Strawbridge had done when he wrote in April, 1801, "The settlement at Pipe Creek is the richest in the state; here Mr. Strawbridge formed the first society in Maryland—and America."

Two hundred eleven years ago today 10 persons were attending the first conference of Methodist preachers in the New World.

Robert Strawbridge

John George Pfrimmer

July 22

A Frenchman made a significant contribution to our early heritage. Dr. John George Pfrimmer was born in France on July 24, 1762. He studied medicine and became a physician and surgeon. He served for a time in the French navy. His battle scars included a saber cut across his face.

Dr. Pfrimmer immigrated to the New World in 1783 and settled in Pennsylvania. In 1790 he was converted and began preaching. He attended the conference in 1800 when the United Brethren in Christ Church was formed and Philip William Otterbein and Martin Boehm were elected superintendents.

In 1808 Dr. Pfrimmer moved to Corydon, Indiana. He became recognized as an able physician, judge, musician, and preacher. He took an active part in the establishment of a county and state government. William Henry Harrison appointed him probate judge, and he held the position for three years. Pfrimmer and Harrison undertook some business ventures, but they were unsuccessful.

Pfrimmer's Church, the first United Brethren Church in Indiana, was organized in 1812 by Dr. Pfrimmer, and it still exists. In 1813 he organized two more churches and the following year yet another two churches. During his lifetime he organized at least fifteen churches.

Dr. Pfrimmer was also a pioneer in the church school emphasis. He gathered children in his own home to teach them.

This week we honor Dr. Pfrimmer and others like him who pioneered in the establishment of churches and/or church schools.

Asbury Visits a Black Congregation

July 29

On November 29, 1758, John Wesley baptized two slaves; it was the first time he had baptized blacks. He wrote in his *Journal,* "I rode to Wandsworth, and baptized two negroes belonging to Nathaniel Gilbert, a gentleman lately from Antigua. One of these is deeply convinced of sin; the other rejoices in God her Saviour, and is the first African Christian I have known."

These African Christians and their master are generally credited with introducing Methodism in Antigua. By 1796, Dr. Coke reported that the West Indian Mission had more than ten thousand members.

The earliest black evangelist in the colonies was a volunteer servant to Francis Asbury named Harry Hosier, or "Black Harry." When Asbury preached indoors, an overflow crowd often gathered outside. Hosier preached to those outdoors.

On such an occasion, Hosier was preaching outdoors in Wilmington, Delaware, when two men passing by took notice. One man commented, "I can see why that Asbury is a bishop."

The friend responded, "That's not the bishop; that's his servant."

The first man concluded, "If that is the servant, what must the master be!"

One of the oldest continuing Black United Methodist churches in the United States is Zoar United Methodist Church in Philadelphia. The congregation met in a butcher shop until the first lot was purchased in 1794. Francis Asbury wrote in his *Journal* on August 4, 1796, "I was called upon by the African Society in Campington [a section of Philadelphia] to open their new church."

There have been many heartbreaks for ethnic minority persons within our denomination, but hopefully our quadrennial emphasis on the ethnic minority local church is contributing to a brighter future for the diversity of persons within The United Methodist Church.

We affirm that diversity and celebrate today the invitation extended to Francis Asbury to be present at the opening of the Zoar Church in Philadelphia 188 years ago this week.

Harry Hosier

Camp Meetings

August 5

The camp meeting was used for three generations by our spiritual ancestors. From 1790 to 1810 camp meetings were widely held in frontier areas.

People came to a site in wagons. Families brought their own provisions and stayed for days and sometimes weeks. Crude pulpits were erected, and services were held several times a day. Peter Cartwright said it was not unusual for as many as three to seven men to preach from different stands at the same time.

The Long-Calm camp meeting in Maryland was held from the 8th to the 14th of October in 1806 and reported 580 converts. In August, 1813, Francis Asbury reported that three thousand people were at a camp ground in Pennsylvania. In 1809, seventeen camp meetings were held on the Indiana District of the Western Conference. Asbury wrote of those meetings, "I hear and see the great effects produced by them, and this year there will be more than ever." There was a time when practically every district held such gatherings, usually in the fall of the year.

Halford Luccock wrote the following evaluation, "It was inevitable that there were emotional excesses, but they were not generally encouraged, and the permanent good far exceeded any evils. The camp meeting was a great factor in the spread of the church on the advancing frontier."

Philip Embury

August 12

Immigrants from Ireland were responsible for starting Methodism in New York City. Barbara Heck and her husband and Peter Embury and his wife were among the immigrants who arrived in New York City in the middle of August, 1760.

Philip Embury was a carpenter and had been converted on Christmas day of 1752. He was made a class leader and became a local preacher in 1758. Two years later he ended his work in Ireland and immigrated to New York.

The first six years in New York were difficult and apparently Embury was inactive in religious endeavors. Finally Barbara Heck, his cousin, confronted him, exclaiming, "You must preach to us, or we shall all go to hell, and God will require our blood at your hands!"

"Where shall I preach?" he asked. "How can I preach, for I have neither a house nor a congregation?"

"Preach in your own house and to your own company first," she replied.

In the fall of 1766 Embury held the first service in his home with a congregation of five persons (including an African servant). The congregation soon outgrew Embury's house, so an empty room was rented near some British barracks. Within two years they built the first Methodist church in New York City, and dedicated it to the glory of God on October 30, 1768.

It was 224 years ago this week that the Emburys and their companions arrived in New York City.

Birth of Francis Asbury

August 19

Francis Asbury, one of the great persons in religious history, was born August 20 or 21, 1745, near Birmingham, England. He was the son of a gardener. We are told that his mother had a vision that her unborn baby would be a spiritual leader. In his early years she read to him from the Bible for an hour each day and taught him hundreds of hymns. Years later he read through the Bible three times each year and was so familiar with it that he could name chapter and verse for any text he might need.

Francis Asbury did poorly in school, yet later, as an adult, he taught himself Latin, Hebrew, and Greek.

As a youth he was apprenticed to a blacksmith (good training for a person who would ride 265,000 miles on horseback). The blacksmith who trained him later came to America also, established a business, and helped build Foundry Methodist Church in Washington, D.C.

In his early teens Asbury had a religious awakening and at seventeen he began lay preaching. He was admitted to the British Conference in 1768. At the annual conference in 1771 Wesley made a plea for America and asked, "Who will go?" Asbury was twenty-six years old; for several months he had thought about going to America. After much prayer he volunteered. He was accepted and was appointed for that mission.

Asbury became the leader of American Methodism. When he arrived in 1771, there were approximately a dozen preachers and no more than a thousand Methodists in societies. When he died in 1816, there were 695 preachers and 214,000 Methodists in nine annual conferences.

This week we celebrate the 239th anniversary of the birth of Francis Asbury.

Birth of Peter Cartwright

August 26

Peter Cartwright (1785-1872) was one of the unique persons in United Methodist history. Physically big and strong with a keen wit and quick tongue, he became a legend within a short span of time.

One of the many stories about him refers to an incident which took place in Kentucky. A tavern was kept by a notorious bully. His loud and repeated boast was, "No preacher gets past here." Peter Cartwright was riding circuit that way. He had heard of the man's boast, but he kept riding. News of the arrival of the circuit rider was carried to the tavern keeper, who came out as he saw Cartwright coming. The tavern keeper ordered Cartwright to turn around. Cartwright got off his horse and a fight developed. Cartwright soon had the tavern keeper on the ground. During the fight Cartwright sang "All Hail the Power of Jesus' Name." Within three verses the tavern keeper promised to stop interfering with the preachers.

In his autobiography, Peter Cartwright told of the growth of Methodism during the first twenty years of his ministry (from 1804-1824). The number of members had grown from 113,000 to 329,000. The number of preachers had grown from 400 to 1,272.

Cartwright described the Methodist preacher of his early years,

> A Methodist preacher in those days, when he felt that God had called him to preach . . . hunted up a hardy pony of a horse, and some traveling apparatus, and with his library always at hand, namely, Bible, Hymn-Book, and Discipline, he started, and with a text that never wore out nor grew stale, he cried, 'Behold the Lamb of God, that taketh away the sin of the world.' In this way he went through storms of wind, hail, snow, and rain; climbed hills and mountains, traversed valleys, plunged through swamps, swam swollen streams, lay out all night, wet, weary, and hungry,

held his horse by the bridle all night, or tied him to a limb, slept with his saddle blanket for a bed. . . . Often he slept in dirty cabins, on earthen floors, before the fire. . . . This was old-fashioned Methodist preacher fare and fortune.

This week we celebrate the birth of Peter Cartwright, who was born on September 1, 1785—199 years ago.

Asbury Sails from Europe

September 2

September 4, 1771. Francis Asbury sailed from Bristol, England, for the New World. A few weeks earlier he had volunteered at a conference of Methodist preachers to go to the New World. At last he and Richard Wright set sail on a voyage that would last fifty-five days.

Asbury started a *Journal* in preparation for the trip. That *Journal* extended to several volumes, and the last entry was dated December 7, 1815, (which was approximately four months before he died).

In the forty-four years covered by those *Journals* we have preserved for us a record of the life of Asbury—constant travels, ill health, hardships of various kinds, worship services in a wide variety of places. The *Journals* also provide a record of the growth and development of Methodism on this continent.

From those *Journals* we learn that Asbury traveled more than 265,000 miles on horseback. He crossed the Allegheny Mountains sixty times. He preached sixteen thousand sermons, an average of one a day for forty-four years.

On the voyage to the New World he tried to examine his motives for coming and wrote, "Whither am I going? To the New World. What to do? To gain honour? No, if I know my own heart. To get money? No: I am going to live to God and to bring others so to do. . . . "

Asbury also wrote, "I want faith, courage, patience, meekness, love. . . . I feel my spirit bound to the New World, and my heart united to the people."

Francis Asbury started to the shores of this land 213 years ago this week.

Thomas Coke

Birth of Thomas Coke

September 9

Two hundred thirty-seven years ago today a person was born who became a missionary light to his age. His name was Thomas Coke, born on September 9, 1747, at Brecon in Wales. He went to Oxford to school and graduated there in 1770. In learning and culture he was the equal of any clergyman of his time. He became a priest in the Church of England and became a Methodist when he was thirty years of age.

Thomas Coke was sent by John Wesley to organize the Methodists in the New World into a new denomination. He and Francis Asbury were to become the first two superintendents.

While he acted as a superintendent here, he had charge also of the Irish Conference and presided over it more than John Wesley himself. In the fulfillment of his responsibilities he crossed the Atlantic Ocean eighteen times.

Though he made nine trips here, he spent only a total of three years in this country. Yet those years were packed. He could ride a horse as far as anyone else and preach as often.

He was an outspoken opponent against slavery. On several occasions he was mobbed for his protests against it. Coke and Asbury visited George Washington at Mount Vernon to try to get him to sign a petition against slavery; Washington agreed to sign the petition if the General Assembly of Virginia took the matter under consideration.

Coke died in 1814 while on board the *Cabalva* on the way to India. Halford Luccock and Paul Hutchinson wrote of him:

> Before the days of William Carey, Coke was possessed with a consuming zeal for foreign missions. He proposed a mission to India before Carey and Thomas went out in 1793. As early as January, 1784, he had framed 'A plan for the establishment of

Missions among the Heathen,' and his name led the subscribers for its support. It was a poetic culmination of his life that its last enterprise should be the organization of a mission of the Wesleyan Church of England to go to India and that just at the threshold of that work he should die at sea.

John Dickins

September 16

Every organization needs an idea person, and John Dickins was the idea person for the early Methodists.

Dickins was born in England and educated at Eton College. He came to the New World and became one of our early leaders.

Prior to the Christmas Conference John Dickins had tried to persuade Asbury to start a school. Asbury thought it should be an elementary school. Coke insisted upon a college. At the Christmas Conference in 1784, the group decided upon a college. It was probably Dickins who suggested the name of Cokesbury.

Dickins is definitely credited for suggesting "Methodist Episcopal Church" as the name of the denomination formed at the Christmas Conference.

John Dickins was also among the group of four who visited George Washington within a month after his inauguration as president. It is thought that the Methodists were the first religious group to declare its loyalty to the new government.

In 1789 the Methodist Book Concern was organized. John Dickins was appointed as book steward. Since no money was appropriated for the task, John Dickins volunteered his own life's savings and with that $600 undertook the new venture in Philadelphia. The first book published was John Wesley's translation of Thomas à Kempis' *The Imitation of Christ.* The Book Concern supplied the books and tracts for the circuit riders who became the "bookmobiles" of their time.

September was an important month in the life of John Dickins. On Saturday, September 16, 1786, he was ordained a minister by Francis Asbury (that was 198 years ago today). He died on September 27, 1798, in Philadelphia in an epidemic of yellow fever. He was an ordained minister for only twelve years but was an influential person in Methodism's early days.

The United Brethren Organize

September 23

In June we reviewed the occasion when Philip Otterbein and Martin Boehm met. They continued to work and preach in various communities. They reached many persons and discovered others to preach who shared their viewpoint and mission, particularly in reaching those who spoke German. The number of followers grew, especially in the states of Pennsylvania, Maryland, and Virginia.

In 1789 a conference was held in the city of Baltimore at which seven preachers were present. At a similar conference in 1791 nine preachers were present. Finally they decided to form a separate denomination.

Thus they met on September 25, 1800, at the house of Frederick Kemp in Frederick County, Maryland. Thirteen preachers attended. They bound themselves in a group which they called the United Brethren in Christ, and elected William Otterbein and Martin Boehm as superintendents.

At a conference in Westmoreland County, Pennsylvania, in 1815, the denomination drew up a *Book of Discipline,* containing the doctrines and rules of the church.

The paths of the German-speaking evangelists and the English-speaking Methodists crossed often. It would be 1968 before a merger would take place, but from the earliest days there was much respect between the groups. After the death of Otterbein, Francis Asbury conducted a service in memory of him, during the session of the Methodist Baltimore Annual Conference. In his eulogy, Asbury said, "Forty years have I known the retiring modesty of this man of God: towering majestic above his fellows in learning, wisdom, and grace, yet seeking to be known only of God and the people of God."

It was 184 years ago this week that the United Brethren in Christ denomination was officially formed.

Christian Newcomer

September 30

What would you expect of a person named Christian Newcomer? See if the story of the life of the man matches his name.

Newcomer came from a Mennonite background and was reared in a religious home. In time he withdrew from the Mennonite Church and joined with Otterbein and Boehm. He was present at the organizational meeting of the United Brethren in Christ in 1800.

He preached for thirty years before he was ordained, but finally he received ordination on October 2, 1813. Prior to his ordination he had been elected a bishop.

Christian Newcomer moved the United Brethren toward formal organization (many persons of Mennonite background were opposed because they thought the Bible alone was sufficient). In the general conference of 1815, the body approved the publication of a Discipline but did not formally adopt it. The second general conference which met in 1817 modified the Discipline, and this time it was officially adopted. Thus, through tact and persistence, Christian Newcomer gained a rule book for the organization.

Newcomer was on the move as a minister for thirty-five years and served as a bishop for seventeen years. Dr. A. W. Drury wrote of him,

> He gathered the first missionary money, and was noted for the number of young men that he introduced into the ministry. He preached, for the most part, in German, but also in English. He opened the way for a larger fellowship with kindred denominations, laboring even for an organic union of the United Brethren and Evangelical Association.

The name was appropriate for the man, and so we celebrate the ordination of Christian Newcomer as a minister 171 years ago this week.

Jason Lee to Oregon

October 7

Four Indians from Oregon appeared in St. Louis in the latter part of 1831. The Indians asked about the white man's God and their book about God, the Bible. Since a Bible had not been written in their language and they could not read English, what they really needed was a missionary.

No immediate help was given. The Indians were disappointed. In a speech one of them said,

> You make my feet heavy with gifts, and my moccasins will grow old in carrying them, and yet the Book is not among them! When I tell my poor blind people, after one more snow, in the big council, that I did not bring the Book, no word will be spoken by our old men or by our young braves. One by one, they will rise up and go out in silence. My people will die in darkness, and they will go on a long path to other hunting-grounds. No white man will go with them, and no white man's Book to make the way plain. I have no more words.

The words were published. Jason Lee learned of the challenge and answered the call to go to Oregon. It was two and one-half years after the Indians had appeared in St. Louis that Jason Lee arrived. He was thirty-one years old when he settled near what is now Salem, Oregon. Jason Lee preached the first Protestant sermon on the Pacific coast on September 28, 1834.

In later years, Lee returned to the East to encourage people to migrate to Oregon and to encourage the government to negotiate with Great Britain so that the area could come under American control. That agreement was finally reached in 1846.

One hundred fifty years ago this October Jason Lee began his first full month as a missionary in Oregon.

Tribute to Asbury

October 14

A statue of Francis Asbury on horseback was unveiled in Washington, D.C., on October 15, 1924. It is located north out 16th street, just beyond Columbia Road, and is one of the few statues in Washington that does not pertain to the government or military.

Listen to what Hartzell Spence wrote of this early leader of American Methodism:

> He spread and nurtured the early seeds of Methodism throughout America. A tireless rider, he helped organize conferences and the previously spotty Sunday-school programs. And he presided over the conference at which the Methodist Publishing House . . . was born.
>
> He encouraged church women to emancipate themselves by charting their tireless energies into noble causes; he started the first organized campaigns against slavery and the liquor traffic. He trained and sent out the circuit riders who, most historians agree, became the most potent force in civilizing the frontier. And he organized a scattered band of 1,000 Methodists into a church which, at his death, numbered 210,000 members.
>
> All this Asbury accomplished without any of the usual attributes of great leadership. He was no glamour boy, no spellbinder, no organization man, and he was plagued all his adult life by illness so dire that for 15 years he expected every day to be his last. Call him zealot or saint; but name him great. Few men have accomplished so much with so little education and physical endowment.

* * *

Historians say he rode horseback perhaps farther than any man in American history . . . averaging 6,000 miles a year or some 265,000 miles in 44 years. Visiting every Methodist preacher in America every year, he had a schedule so tight that he could sleep only six hours a night, lest he be late to an appointment.

* * *

Many epitaphs have been written for "the prophet of the long road," but only one has ever succinctly summed him up. It was written by his fellow preacher, Freeborn Garrettson, and says, "He prayed the best, and prayed the most, of any man I ever knew."

Francis Asbury

Richard Boardman and Joseph Pilmoor

October 21

In the year 1769 John Wesley received correspondence from American Methodist laypersons stating that they wanted some ordained Methodist ministers from England. The laypersons in America wrote they would "sell their coats and shirts", if need be, to pay the passage of the preachers to the New World.

At the conference of his preachers, which met at Leeds, England, Wesley told of the need in the "wilderness of America." He asked who would be willing to go. Richard Boardman and Joseph Pilmoor volunteered.

However their response was not spontaneous. Joseph Pilmoor himself records that he had thought about it ahead of time. He had come to the conference determined to offer himself for America, but he did not immediately respond. He thought about it some more before offering himself.

Pilmoor and Boardman set sail on August 21 and arrived in Pennsylvania on October 24, 1769, (215 years ago this week). They started their work as Pilmoor preached from the steps of the state house.

Pilmoor was thirty when he arrived in the New World; Boardman was thirty-one. Boardman began his ministry in New York City. Three months later, Boardman moved to Philadelphia and Pilmoor went to New York. They swapped appointments every three months. Under their leadership Methodism grew rapidly.

In 1774 both Pilmoor and Boardman returned to England. Years later, Pilmoor returned to America. However he took orders in the Protestant Episcopal Church and served as rector in New York and Philadelphia. At the conference of 1804 Francis Asbury introduced him as "Brother Pilmoor, who used to preach . . . under the direction of Mr. John Wesley."

New York City Church

October 28

Earlier we mentioned the beginning of Methodism in New York City under the leadership of Philip Embury, a lay preacher. Five persons had been present at the first service. They soon moved their services to a room in the neighborhood of the British barracks. The singing of the Methodists was different from that of other churches and attracted to the meetings some of the musicians in the regimental bands. Two of them were converted and began to preach.

One day a captain in the British army appeared for the service. His name was Thomas Webb. He had been a preacher for John Wesley. He had lost his right eye in the siege of Louisburg; in the battle of Quebec he had been wounded in his right arm.

Captain Webb began preaching in the New York congregation. John Adams, who later became president of the United States, heard him preach and wrote of him as "one of the most eloquent men I ever heard; he reaches the imagination and touches the passions very well, and expresses himself with great propriety."

Because of increased attendance the congregation moved once more—to the "Rigging Loft" where sails had been made. From there the group decided to build their own church. A lot was selected in the spring of 1768 on John Street. Philip Embury supervised the construction. The church became known as Wesley Chapel.

On October 30, 1768, (216 years ago this week) Philip Embury preached the dedicatory sermon for the new church. He preached from the pulpit he had made with his own hands.

The name of the church has changed; it is now called John Street Church, but its activity has not lapsed across the years. It is now located in the heart of the Wall Street business district of New York City.

Old "Wesley Chapel," John Street, New York

Jacob Albright

November 4

Jacob Albright was born in Montgomery County, Pennsylvania, on May 1, 1759, and was brought up as a Lutheran. He joined the army during the Revolutionary War. After the war he married and earned a livelihood as a farmer and a tile maker. The Albrights became the parents of nine children.

An epidemic struck in 1790, and several of the children died. Albright wondered if God were punishing him. The next year he attended a prayer meeting; later he wrote about it, "I was converted deep into eternal life."

He began meeting with others. The first steps toward organization were taken when in 1800 three classes were formed. All three were in Pennsylvania.

On November 3, 1803, (181 years ago yesterday), people from five areas came together and granted Albright a certification which read, "We, the undersigned, as evangelical and Christian friends, declare Jacob Albright as a truly evangelical minister in every sense of the word and deed, and a professor in the universal Christian Church and the communion of saints." Thus his ordination was bestowed by lay persons.

The first conference after that was held on November 13, 1807, at the home of Samuel Becker, a farmer who lived near Kleinfeltersville, Pennsylvania. Albright was elected to superintend the organization that they named "The Newly-Formed Methodist Conference." Albright died the next year at the age of forty-nine, and eight years later the name of the church was changed to The Evangelical Association.

In November, 1946, the United Brethren Church and the Evangelical Church joined together to form the Evangelical United Brethren Church. In 1968 the Evangelical United Brethren Church merged with The Methodist Church to form The United Methodist Church.

Barrett's Chapel

November 11

As a result of the American Revolution John Wesley in England realized that the Methodists in America needed to be a separate denomination. In February, 1784, Mr. Wesley called in Dr. Thomas Coke, one of his British Methodist preachers, and disclosed his plan to organize the Methodists in America into a separate denomination and to make Thomas Coke and Francis Asbury (who was already in America) the first two bishops of the new denomination. Dr. Coke asked for time to think the matter through before he could become a party to the plan.

Five months later Mr. Wesley divulged his idea to a selected group of British Methodist preachers. According to the report of one of those preachers, they were all opposed to the idea. One of the ministers who was present wrote, "I plainly saw that it would be done, as Mr. Wesley's mind was quite made up."

Dr. Coke was at last persuaded. Thus seven months after Mr. Wesley had originally proposed the plan, Dr. Coke boarded a ship for the New World. With him were two other British preachers, Richard Whatcoat and Thomas Vasey.

Upon arrival in New York Dr. Coke wanted to find Francis Asbury, but Asbury was on a circuit in Delaware. Dr. Coke started to Delaware, taking time to preach as he made his way southward.

Two hundred years ago this week, on November 14, 1784, Thomas Coke preached in a plain brick building near Dover, Delaware, known as Barrett's Chapel. The church was jammed. As Dr. Coke gave the benediction he saw a man making his way to the pulpit. The man clasped him in his arms. At last Coke had found Francis Asbury.

Later that day Dr. Coke made known the plan of Mr. Wesley. Asbury agreed to a meeting of the preachers to decide the issue.

They assigned Freeborn Garrettson the responsibility to travel all across the colonies to get the message to every Methodist preacher. They would meet on Christmas Eve at Lovely Lane Chapel in Baltimore and decide what to do about Mr. Wesley's plans.

Philadelphia Church

November 18

The earliest known date for an organized Methodist society in Philadelphia, Pennsylvania, was 1767. A sail loft was the site on Dock Creek. (The Methodists in New York also met at one time in a sail loft.)

When Captain Thomas Webb, a British soldier and lay preacher, arrived from New York, he built the group into a society of seven persons. He continued to preach there until Richard Boardman and Joseph Pilmoor arrived from England in October, 1769.

The group looked for a new meeting place. They found a building which had been a German Reformed Church. That church had gone bankrupt and the property had been sold. In 1769 the owner was willing to sell at a loss. The contract was signed on Thursday, November 23, 1769.

This church became a vital part of our heritage. In this church Francis Asbury preached his first sermon in America on October 28, 1771. In this church were held the first early Christmas morning service (December 25, 1769), the first American Methodist love feast (March 23, 1770), the first three conferences of American Methodism (1773, '74, '75).

John Dickins was pastor of this church when he organized the Methodist Book Concern (now The Methodist Publishing House).

The congregation is now known as St. George's Church and is the oldest continuous Methodist church in the United States. The building is part of Independence National Historical Park.

Two hundred fifteen years ago this week the dedication service was held for the new church building in Philadelphia.

Black Missionaries

November 25

The first home missionary in the Methodist Episcopal Church was John Stewart, a free-born mulatto born in Virginia. In his young adulthood he became an alcoholic and thought of committing suicide. However in 1815 he was converted in a camp meeting. Later he felt a voice speak to him, "Thou shalt declare my counsel faithfully."

Soon he decided to go as a missionary to the Indians. Taking with him his Bible and hymn book, he preached and sang hyms in an appealing, melodious voice.

He went even though he had no authorization and no guaranteed support. He worked first with the Delaware Indians. His first congregation consisted of two persons. In November, 1816, he began his formal ministry with the Wyandotte Indians. His work grew so that when Bishop William McKendree visited the mission in 1822 the membership totaled two hundred persons. Stewart died of tuberculosis in 1823 which meant his ministry was limited to but seven years.

The first Black missionaries sent out from America by the United Brethren Board of Missions were Mr. and Mrs. Joseph Gomer. They had been in Sierra Leone less than a year when Gomer faced two hostile groups who were led by cousins who had been bitter enemies. Mr. Gomer told one chief that he had wronged his cousin and his cousin's people. He then told the second chief he had been unjust to his relative and his relative's people. After Gomer had lectured them he said, "You have seen what comes from war. Why not try peace?"

What would happen? After a moment's silence came shouts of joy. People crowded around. The chiefs had agreed to try the new way of peace.

Today we celebrate our mission work and the people who make for peace.

Isaac Owen and Thomas Taylor in California

December 2

Gold was discovered in California in 1848. Two years later—by the end of 1849—77,000 fortune hunters had thronged into the Mother Lode country. Methodist preachers went too.

One of those Methodist preachers was Isaac Owen. He traveled overland by covered wagon and arrived in the fall of 1849. On his first Sunday in Grass Valley, California, he stuck his cane in the ground and placed his hat on it for a pulpit, and preached.

Isaac Owen earned the title of the "knight of the saddlebags." He organized churches, insisted that members keep their records correctly, and collected gold dust for churches and a university (now the University of the Pacific).

Another one of the Methodist preachers who went to California was William Taylor. He arrived by ship at San Francisco and preached his first street sermon on December 3, 1849. His efforts were regarded by most people as dangerous since the gamblers were a powerful and influential part of the city and Sunday was the best day of the week for doing business.

Owen and Taylor got together and built the first continuing bookstore in California; that bookstore housed about two thousand dollars worth of books that Owen had collected in the East.

Owen continued his work until his death at the age of fifty-seven. Taylor stayed for several years in California, but then went on to Australia and South Africa. He arrived in India in 1870 and began to lay foundations there. In 1884 he was elected a missionary bishop of Africa and continued his work on that continent for twelve years.

Today we celebrate the beginning of our efforts in California. It was 135 years ago that Isaac Owen preached his first sermon there, and the anniversary comes this week of that first sermon William Taylor preached in San Francisco.

Freeborn Garrettson

December 9

In 1784 John Wesley dispatched Dr. Thomas Coke to America with instructions to organize Methodism in the New World. When Dr. Coke and Francis Asbury got together in this land on November 14, they decided to get all the preachers together to determine what should be done.

There were eighty-one Methodist preachers in North America at that time. Freeborn Garrettson was dispatched to contact the ministers. The majority of them were in remote rural areas of Virginia and what is now the Carolinas, Georgia, and Pennsylvania. It had taken a month for the news of the signing of the Declaration of Independence to travel from Philadelphia to Charlestown, South Carolina. It would take hard riding for Garrettson to cover the distances, notify the preachers, and give them a few days to get to Baltimore by Christmas Eve.

On his journey to fulfill his mission, Freeborn Garrettson traveled approximately twelve hundred miles in about six weeks. Jesse Lee, the first Methodist historian, said that Garrettson's love of preaching slowed him down. He failed to get the message to some preachers in western Pennsylvania.

It was an arduous trip. Later Garrettson was called the "Paul Revere of Methodism."

Garrettson's early ministry included Maryland, Virginia, the Carolinas, Pennsylvania, Delaware, and New Jersey. Later he became a famous evangelist in Nova Scotia. He returned to Maryland and then was appointed to the territory above New York City. His ministry covered a span of fifty years. Yet he is known most today for his famous ride, and he was on that ride 200 years ago this week.

Planning for Christmas Conference

December 16

In 1784 John Wesley sent Dr. Thomas Coke to the United States to organize the Methodists in this country. Dr. Coke met with Francis Asbury on November 14, and they agreed to call a conference of the preachers to meet on Christmas Eve in Baltimore.

After meeting with Asbury, Coke set off on a thousand-mile preaching tour through Delaware, Virginia, and Maryland—the Eastern Shore.

Asbury needed time to think about the plan to form a new denomination. For a whole day he prayed and fasted. Then he noted in his *Journal* that he believed Wesley's plan was "of the Lord."

On December 14 Coke and Asbury met again and spent several days planning for the upcoming conference. At the same time other preachers were learning of the conference and heading for Baltimore.

At the conference Thomas Haskins, a former law student, wanted to proceed cautiously with the new plan. He wrote out his opinion and recommended that the preachers wait until a second conference to make a decision. He wanted preachers to talk with American leaders in what had been the Church of England to get their opinions of the situation. He felt they should give long consideration to staying within the successor to the Church of England.

The idea Thomas Haskins presented to the Conference indicates some serious thinking was being done as the preachers made their way toward Baltimore two hundred years ago today.

Christmas Conference Convened

December 23

The Christmas Conference convened on December 24, 1784. Sixty-three of the eighty Methodist preachers in the United States were present. This shows how little Christmas was observed by the Methodist preachers.

The preachers had been summoned into special session. They had been scheduled to meet the following June, but instructions from Mr. Wesley told them to organize immediately.

They met in Baltimore in Lovely Lane Chapel, which was only ten years old. The church was refitted for the impending sessions. A gallery was put in to accommodate visitors who would observe the proceedings. A stove was installed. Some of the rude benches had backs pegged onto them. Thus they were made to resemble pews, though Mr. Wesley had once laid down an explicit rule that seats should not have backs.

The preachers who attended the conference were a youthful group. Most of them were in their twenties. Thomas Coke was thirty-seven, and Francis Asbury was thirty-nine.

The conference was convened at ten o'clock in the morning. The preachers voted to establish the Methodist Episcopal Church. The conference also voted to make Dr. Thomas Coke and Francis Asbury general superintendents. Since Asbury had never been ordained, he was ordained a deacon one day, an elder a second day, and consecrated a superintendent on a third day.

The Christmas Conference lasted a week. When it was over, Methodism was officially organized in the new nation. This historic conference began 200 years ago tomorrow.

The Christmas Conference

December 30

Two hundred years ago today the Methodist preachers of this nation were in the midst of a historic conference. As mentioned last Sunday, the Methodists organized themselves into The Methodist Episcopal Church during the Christmas Conference. Dr. Thomas Coke and Francis Asbury were elected general superintendents. Thus Methodism became the first nationally-organized church in the United States of America.

Also at this conference, several persons were ordained as ministers. The ritual which was adopted was an edited and abridged form of the order of service used in the Church of England.

Preaching services were held three times a day. Dr. Coke preached at the noon services and others preached in the morning and evening services.

During the conference the preachers gave Mr. Wesley this pledge, "During the life of the Reverend Mr. Wesley, we acknowledge ourselves his Sons in the Gospel, ready in matters belonging to church-government, to obey his commands." However three years later in 1787 when Mr. Wesley tried to exert some authority over the new denomination, he discovered the group was now charting its own course. They gladly followed his interpretation of scripture, yet they felt they knew better than he what kind of church government was best suited for this country.

When the Christmas Conference was over, the preachers returned to their appointments. They and their successors did their work so well that within seventy-five years Methodism was the number one Protestant denomination in this country.

Bibliography

Anderson, William K., ed. *Methodism.* Cincinnati: Methodist Publishing House, 1947.

Applegarth, Margaret T. *Twelve Baskets Full.* New York: Harper, 1957.

Asbury, Francis. *Journal.*

Barclay, Wade Crawford. *Early American Methodism 1769-1844.* Vol. 1, *Missionary Motivation and Expansion.* New York: Board of Missions and Church Extension of the Methodist Church, 1949.

Behney, J. Bruce, and Paul H. Eller. *The History of the Evangelical United Brethren Church.* Edited by Kenneth W. Krueger. Nashville: Abingdon, 1979.

Bonner, Clint. *A Hymn Is Born.* Nashville: Broadman, 1959.

Bucke, Emory Stevens, ed. *The History of American Methodism.* 3 vols. New York: Abingdon, 1964.

Cain, J. B. *Methodism in the Mississippi Conference, 1846-1870.* Jackson, Miss.: Hawkins Foundation, 1939.

Carter, Henry. *The Methodist Heritage.* London: Epworth, 1951.

Cartwright, Peter. *Autobiography of Peter Cartwright, the Backwoods Preacher.* Edited by W. P. Strickland. Cincinnati: Cranston and Curts, 1856.

Condo, Adam Byron. *History of the Indiana Conference of the Church of the United Brethren in Christ.* N.p.: Indiana Conference, 1926.

Duren, William Larkin. *Trail of the Circuit Rider.* New Orleans: Chalmers, 1936.

Eller, Paul Himmel. *These Evangelical United Brethren.* Dayton, Ohio: Otterbein, 1950.

Ensley, Francis Gerald. *John Wesley, Evangelist.* Nashville: Methodist Evangelistic Materials, 1958.

Evangelical United Brethren Church. *The Discipline of the Evangelical United Brethren Church.* Dayton, Ohio: Otterbein, 1947.

Ferguson, Charles W. *Organizing to Beat the Devil; Methodists and the Making of America.* Garden City, N.Y.: Doubleday, 1971.

Fitchett, W. H. *Wesley and His Century; A Study in Spiritual Forces.* New York: Abingdon, 1917.

Garrison, Webb B., and John K. Bergland. *Strangely Warm: The Story of United Methodism.* Nashville: Graded Press, 1971.

Graham, J. H. *Black United Methodists: Retrospect and Prospect.* New York: Vantage, 1979.

Hale, Harry, Jr., Morton King and Doris Moreland Jones. *New Witnesses: United Methodist Clergywomen.* Nashville: Division of Ordained Ministry, Board of Higher Education and Ministry, 1980.

Harmon, Rebecca Lamar. *Susanna: Mother of the Wesleys*. Nashville: Abingdon, 1968.

Hawkins, Henry G. *Methodism in Natchez*. Jackson, Miss.: Hawkins Foundation, 1937.

Heller, Herbert. *Indiana Conference of the Methodist Church 1832-1956*. N.p.: Historical Society of Indiana Conference, 1957.

Hudson, Winthrop S. *Religion in America*. New York: Scribner, 1965.

Jones, George Hawkins. *The Methodist Tourist Guidebook through the 50 States*. Nashville: Tidings, 1966.

Jones, William Burwell. *Methodism in the Mississippi Conference 1870-1894*. Jackson, Miss.: Hawkins Foundation, 1951.

Joy, James Richard. *John Wesley's Awakening*. Dallas: Methodist Publishing House, 1937.

Lee, Jesse. *A Short History of the Methodists, in the United States of America*. Baltimore: Magill and Clime, 1810.

Lee, Umphrey. *John Wesley and Modern Religion*. Nashville: Cokesbury, 1936.

Lee, Umphrey. *The Lord's Horseman*. New York: Century Co., 1928.

Luccock, Halford E. *Endless Line of Splendor*. Chicago: Advance for Christ and His Church, 1950.

Luccock, Halford E., and Paul Hutchinson. *The Story of Methodism*. New York: Methodist Book Concern, 1926.

McTyeire, Holland N. *A History of Methodism*. Nashville: Southern Methodist Publishing House, 1885.

Rattenbury, J. Ernest. *Wesley's Legacy to the World*. Nashville: Cokesbury, 1928.

Selecman, Charles C., and George H. Jones. *The Methodist First Reader, "On Being a Christian."* Nashville: Methodist Evangelistic Materials, 1958.

Sweet, William Warren. *Methodism in American History*. New York: Abingdon, 1953.

Tipple, Ezra Squier. *Francis Asbury—The Prophet of the Long Road*. New York: Methodist Book Concern, 1916.

Walker, Williston. *A History of the Christian Church*. New York: Scribner, 1952.

Wesley, John. *The Journal of John Wesley*. Edited by Percy Livingston Parker, Chicago. Moody, 1952.